Empowering The Less Educated

-

Jack's Curated Business Idea

-

Jack Lookman

Empowering The Less Educated

Jack's Curated Business Idea

Copyright © 2024 Jack Lookman Limited

A. ACKNOWLEDGEMENT

I'm continuously grateful to my Creator and Sustainer, for known and unknown favors, blessings and protection.

I appreciate my parents, for being my vehicle of success.

I was fortified with spiritual and academic knowledge and practices; as well as great life skills.

Contributions of John Tosin Adekunle are much appreciated.

I appreciate my siblings, who've supported me directly and indirectly.

My beautiful Tolu Mayowa Tobi you are very much appreciated.

I appreciate all my Teachers, both formal and informal - Thank you very much.

To all those who've added value to me, I say, thank you.

To my Creator and Sustainer: Alhamdu lillahi rabbi alAAalameena.

B. DEDICATION

This piece of work is dedicated to all my family members.

My Late Dad

My Mum

My Siblings

My Children

Ire awawa ri o. (May you find the blessings that you desire)

Ire aje'n jetan (May our Creator and Sustainer grant us everlasting blessings)

CONTENT

Preamble

Does the world sometimes seem unfair?

The rich getting richer...
And the poor getting poorer?

Is the playing field ever level?
Could a positive difference be made?

Could this be in a cost-effective way?
Could this open opportunities?
Could it add value to one and all?
Could the internet be effectively leveraged?
Could it end generational poverty?

Is an idea the first step...
In a journey of many miles?

Could this opportunity be a blue ocean?
And could you enjoy a monopoly?

Could best practice be leveraged?
To bring about prosperity?

Do your thoughts resonate with mine?
And you can't wait to read?

Go on and read...

I've been waiting for you.

Jack's Curated Business Idea
Jack Lookman

For those watching on <u>YouTube</u>, at 'Curated Business Ideas' the video is timestamped for ease of reference.

1. What is the problem?

Let's take my native Nigeria as a case study. A small percentage of the populace is tertiary educated; some aren't educated due to lack of opportunity, poverty, etc. Some end up with low paid jobs such as being drivers, housemaids, cleaners, etc. As a result the quality of life is not optimised. This affects their youth and old age; and the effects could be generational. It impacts family life and society; some may resort to crime. They don't optimise their potential in adulthood, as work consumes them and they get stuck in challenging financial situations. This cycle may be replicated for generations; with the exception of a few, who may get out of it.

2. What is the idea?

- The idea is to create content for the less educated people.
- The content shall be on multiple digital platforms, which could be leveraged for making impact and money
- Content shall be in video or audio formats.
- It shall be in native languages of the end users.
- The content shall add value to their work or business pursuits.
- The content shall be presented in little understandable chunks.
- The content shall be readily accessible via their smartphones or digital devices.

- There shall also be a module on teaching them the basics of accessing the digital content.
- The content shall add great value to them in the short and long term.

3. What are the products?

- The products shall be digital content, to cover the chosen curriculum.
- They shall be for the less educated demographic, in different native languages of choice.
- It's like an online university for the less educated. There could be online tuition for one-to-one or one-to-many.
- This tuition shall be for those who require attention and support; and shall be at additional cost. There could also be one-to-one physical tuition at a much higher cost; and maybe one-to-many physical tuition, again, at additional cost.
- If appropriate, you may also have the content in text, but this won't be a priority.

4. The Process (Thoughts)

Some of the thoughts to consider:
- Market research
- Content creation
- Team
- Delegation

- Outsourcing
- Scope
- Marketing plan
- Minimum viable product
- Costing and pricing
- Monetisation plan
- Platforms
- Investors
- Reinvestment
- Profit Sharing Formula
- Systems and structures
- Automation
- Affiliate Marketing
- Collaborations
- Market research
- Funding
- Etc

5. The Platforms

These could be physical or digital. If physical, there may be a location and human contact. And, of course, there are related costs. If it's digital, it could be via:

- Social media
- Podcast
- Membership site
- Blog
- Etc

6. Format

It could be in multiple formats, such as:

- Text
- Audio
- Video
- In different languages of choice.
- It should also be in simple understandable vocabulary.

7. Language

Most of the demographic might be unable to speak proper English, therefore you may consider their native languages, Pidgin English or alternatives.

8. The Content

It shall mostly be in:

- Audio and video format.
- It shall be presented in little, easy-to-understand modules.
- It shall have practical examples and case studies as necessary.
- It shall be user-friendly.
- Content of choice shall be:
  o Easily accessible
  o In multiple languages
- It shall be updated as necessary

- There shall also be feedback mechanisms in place in order to get the best possible outcomes.

9. Target Audience

The end users shall be:
- Drivers
- Cleaners
- Housemaids
- Uneducated business people
- Artisans
- Etc

10. The Team (business or project)

This shall include:
- The Content Creator
- Entrepreneur
- Marketer
- Translator / Linguist
- Administrator
- Accountant
- Quality Controller
- Human Resources
- Video editor
- Freelancers
- Project manager
- Social media manager

- IT manager
- Educator
- Etc

11. Marketing

You could explore:
- Digital marketing
- Radio marketing
- Influencer marketing
- Television marketing
- Social media marketing
- Referrals
- Word of Mouth
- Affiliate marketing
- Print media marketing
- Email marketing
- Search engine optimisation
- You could explore using a sales funnel
- Etc

12. Sales funnel / mailing list

By virtue of the service that you offer you are likely to get a mighty list of quality contacts. You should have their mobile numbers and or email addresses. You could monetise the mailing list by marketing and re-marketing products and services; both yours and those of third parties. You could create a sales funnel and automate the process. At some point you could make passive recurring income in which case you shall put in minimal ongoing effort and optimise your income.

13. Monetisation

- You could sell the license of your products and services. That is, your content and related software.
- You could do consultancy.
- You could do affiliate marketing.
- You could sell the business
- You could advertise products and services of 3rd parties
- You could have a franchise
- You could do business collaborations.
- You could get sponsors.
- You could sell the private label rights to interested third parties.
- Your digital products could actually be sold as renewable licenses.
- Customers could renew them monthly, quarterly, biannually or annually. There shall be recurring payments to renew access to the content.

14. Payment options

- These could be monthly quarterly, biannually or annually.
- You could also introduce discounts. The more payment, made at a go, the higher the discount. For example, if their purchase is £10, the discount could be 1%. If the purchase is £10-£20, the discount could be 2%. If the purchase is £20-£30, the discount could be 3%; etc.
- You could explore the discount model that suits you. The discount model needs to be determined by the entrepreneur or by the team and such discounts could be automated, such that at the point of purchasing the product or service it automatically calculates the discount for you.

15. Payment Gateways

How will the customers pay?
This could be via payment gateways such as:
- Stripe
- PayPal
- Pioneer
- Flutterwave
- Paystack
- Interswitch
- VoguePay
- Remita
- GTPay
- PayU
- CashEnvoy
- Fliqpay

- OPay
- Squad
- Amplify
- DusuPay
- Or suitable alternatives.

16. Curriculum

What are you going to be teaching this demographics? This shall be at different levels. You might have part of the curriculum at the beginners level, intermediate level and probably at the higher level. It's up to you. Some curriculum ideas are:

- Skills
- Mindset
- Customer services
- Budgeting
- Time management
- People management
- Resource Management
- Networking
- Trade
- Related content
- Costing
- Pricing
- Literacy
- Numeracy

- Effective communication
- Resuscitation
- Risk management
- Health and safety
- Entrepreneurship
- Investment
- Work ethics
- Money management and literacy
- Research skills
- Relevant biographies or Memoir of Role Models
- Etc

- There could also be tests or exams as necessary.
  - These could be automated and could be multiple choice questions.

17. Benefits and Opportunities

- Reduction in crime
- Gainful occupation
- Monetization
- Job creation
- Wealth creation
- Skills enhancement
- Entrepreneurial aspiration
- Increase in GDP
- Increase in tax revenue
- A more educated society

- Improved language skills
- A fairer society
- Improved IT skills
- Inspiration for greater Pursuits
- Empowerment and Inspiration
- Passive income
- Removing customers from generational cycle of poverty
- Exploration of their individual untapped potential
- Improved quality of life of the end users.
- It makes the end user more proficient in their native language.
- The costs shall be affordable
- The products and services shall be easily accessible
- The products and services shall be user-friendly
- The business could be scaled
- The products could be evergreen
- Instant access to the product
- Cost effective marketing

18. Requirements for the Entrepreneur

Some of the requirements include:
- Digital device or devices
- A team
- Relevant skills
- Positive mindset
- Marketing efforts
- Content creation
- Finance

- Profit sharing formula
- App products or products
- Etc

19. Requirements for the customer

- A digital device.
- Willingness to learn
- A positive mindset
- Business related idea or ideas
- Investment in time commitment
- Occupational skills
- Etc

20. Business Plan Considerations

- Team
- Equipment
- Marketing plan
- Market research
- Monetisation plan
- Competitor research
- Product research
- Legalities
- Platforms
- Sales funnel
- Collaboration
- Investors

- Profit sharing formula
- Marketing

21. Skills required by business

- Video editing
- Content creation
- Entrepreneurship
- Outsourcing
- Marketing
- Project management
- Language and translation skills
- Interpersonal skills
- Customer service skills
- Administration skills
- Organisation skills
- Budgeting skills
- Resource management skills
- IT skills
- Communication skills

22. Skills required by end user

- Basic IT skills
- How to use their digital device or devices
- Occupational skills
- Language skills
- Positive mindset

- Reliability
- Etc

23. Threats

- There could be a fight back from those who wish to maintain the status quo
- Competition
- Sabotage
- Litigation
- Technical problems
- Government legislation
- Intellectual theft
- Accessibility
- Affordability
- Lack of interested customers
- Non-accessibility of telecommunications network
- Unmotivated end users
- Etc

24. Legalities

Here are some thoughts to ponder:
- Outline the agreements or contracts
- Include a disclaimer
- Expectation management
- Intellectual rights ownership
- Refund policy terms and condition

- Indemnification
- adherence to general data protection regulation
- adherence to laws of the land
- Etc

25. Costing And Pricing

Some considerations to have in mind are:
- Profit margin
- Cost of resources used
  - Time
  - Effort
  - Money
  - Cost of the team
  - Freelancers
  - Human Resources
  - Office
- Financial investors
- Equipment
- Marketing and advertising
- Strategizing and brainstorming
- Administration
- Information technology
- Website hosting and domain name
- Etc

- Most of these things have related costs; so you need to quantify them when you're doing your costing and pricing.

- You need to do this per product sold.
- And need to know how much you intend to make
- And if you're going to sell the product in bundles. For example, the cost of that bundle will be slightly cheaper than buying them individually; so you're tempting the customer to buy the bundle and the incentive is that it becomes a bit cheaper. Though it will be a bit cheaper for the client you make more profit than selling an individual product.
- The beautiful thing about this business model is that, if you get it right you could actually generate passive income for a very long time.
- It's also very scalable. You could replicate the process in different languages, and for different demographics, and of course for different subjects.

26. Funding

The business may be funded via:
- Your personal savings
- Investors
- Crowdfunding
- Loans
- Collaboration
- Grants
- Family and friends
- Etc

- You could start small and then reinvest in the in the business.
- You could also use a profit sharing formula app for fair compensation of business stakeholders

27. Complementary Products and Services

- You could start a business with one language. For example in Nigeria, you may prioritize Pidgin English, Yoruba, Hausa, Ibo, etc; as those are the major languages.
- You may create content for different niches and different demographics.
- You may collaborate with relevant others.
- You may promote products and services of relevant Brands and monetize via passive affiliate marketing.
- You may also advertise products and services of 3rd parties on your platform.

28. Possible by-products

- You could replicate the process for professional courses.
- You could do courses on life experience.
- You could do academic courses at different levels.
- You could do courses on life coaching.
- You could do courses on marriage, and other life topics
- You could do courses on best practice
- You could do courses on mannerisms
- And courses on cooking
- You could do courses on business etiquettes

- You could become a consultant; and this could open opportunities
- You could do these on your own or collaborate with third parties.

29. Conclusion

A lot of digital educational content is directed at those who are already educated. Those who have a degree, for instance may only account for 5 to 10% of the populace. The majority are less educated. This may be so due to lack of opportunity, poverty, non-enabling environment, poor teaching, etc. By targeting the less educated; apart from adding great value to society you shall also be exploring huge potentials, as long as you offer value at affordable costs, and market adequately.

It could be a financial game-changer for you. You could literally be rich overnight.

The cost outlay is relatively low and the return on investment could be very high. The break-even-point could be attained within a few months or years.

In marketing terms, this curated business idea may be classified as a blue ocean. That is, it's a business idea with probably little or no competition.

30. Disclaimer

We are also affiliate marketers. We promote products and services of third parties and get a discount at no additional cost to you.

The curated business idea on these and our other platforms are born out of creativity, experience, and exposure. You are expected to modify them to suit your needs.

Inasmuch as they are great ideas, they don't guarantee financial success.

There are many determining factors for success to be achieved. You are expected to carry out due diligence before embarking on any entrepreneurial pursuits.

31. Mission

Our mission at Jack Lookman Limited is to empower and Inspire Generations by leveraging the internet.

32. Value?

We hope that you got some value from this content. If so, please feel free to share your thoughts and comments.

You could get more of such, on our different platforms on social media. You could find us on Youtube, Facebook, TikTok, LinkedIn, etc. Just do a search for Jack Lookman or search for curated business idea or Curated Business Ideas.

You could also access content on our websites:

Jack's Empowerment which is a membership site.

Curated Business Ideas - a blog

Jaaloo Puzzles - jaaloopuzzles.com - jaaloo.com
Jack Lookman Limited - jacklookmanlimited.com

We've also written many books. Please search for Jack Lookman's books on the internet.

- You could also join Jack Lookman's community on Facebook.
- We create content
- We mentor
- We do affiliate marketing
- We do business collaborations
- And app development collaborations

- We've authored and published several books on
  - curated business ideas
  - mindset
  - poetry
  - Jaaloo Puzzles
  - Etc

- If you are interested playing an arithmetic number game called Jaaloo Puzzles, it's a very good brain exercise for children, adults, youths and the elderly. It helps with accuracy skills, mental alertness, competition skills, arithmetic and logic skills, etc. You could find it at jaaloo.com and jaaloopuzzles.com

- Are you interested in Business Collaboration With Jack Lookman ?

- Or in Jack's Mentoring 101 ?
- If yes, search for it or them at jacksempowerment.com

If you got some value, kindly consider liking, sharing, subscribing, and reposting via our Social media platforms.

33. Useful compliments

1.Jack's Empowerment - membership site - jacksempowerment.com

2. Jaaloo Puzzles - blog - jaaloopuzzles.com

3. Curated Business Ideas - blog - curatedbusinessideas.com

4. Jack Lookman Limited - blog - jacklookmanlimited.com

5. Youtube channel: Curated Business Ideas

6. Youtube channel: Jaaloo Puzzles

7. Youtube channel: Life Lessons For Teenagers

8. Facebook: Jack Lookman

9. Facebook: Curated Business Ideas

10. Facebook: Jaaloo Puzzles

11. Facebook: Life Lessons For Teenagers

12. Jack Lookman's Books

13. Business Collaboration With Jack Lookman - jacksempowerment.com

14. Jack's Mentoring 101 - jacksempowerment.com

15. Youtube video: Empowering The Less Educated

16. Facebook video: Empowering The Less Educated

34. Useful hashtags

1. #jackscuratedbusinessidea
2. #jackscuratedbusinessideas
3. #JaalooPuzzles
4. #CuratedBusinessIdeas
5. #JackLookmanLimited
6. #ireo
7. #Irekabiti
8. #JackLookman
9. #empoweringandinspiringgenerations
10. #EmpowermentandInspiration

35. Books by Jack Lookman

Visit:

- amazon.co.uk search for Jack Lookman
- https://selar.co/m/jacklookman
- Internet search? Jack Lookman
- Or Jack Lookman's Books

36. Some resources by Jack Lookman

- Jack's Empowerment - jacksempowerment.com
- Jaaloo Puzzles - jaaloopuzzles.com
- Jaaloo Puzzles - jaaloo.com

- Curated Business Ideas curatedbusinessideas.com
- Youtube channel: Jack Lookman - https://youtube.com/@jacklookman
- Youtube channel: Curated Business Ideas
- Facebook: Jack Lookman
- https://www.facebook.com/jack.lookman.3
- Facebook group: Curated Business Ideas
- Facebook group: Menteero
- Facebook group: Jaaloo Puzzles

37. Did you get value?

Did you learn 1 or 2 things? Did it stimulate your thoughts? Could it benefit family or friends?

If yes, please consider liking, sharing, subscribing and reposting content on our Social media platforms.

Also consider purchasing our products and services.

38. Will you like to collaborate?

Does the Jack Lookman brand resonate with you? Will you like to collaborate? If yes, please send an email to: jacklookman@yahoo.co.uk

Use an appropriate subject heading and narrative.

39. Will you like to be mentored by Jack Lookman?

If yes, please send an email to: jacklookman@yahoo.co.uk

Use an appropriate subject heading and narrative.

You could also check our websites:

- Jack's Empowerment: - jacksempowerment.com
- Jaaloo Puzzles - jaaloo.com
- Jack's Mentoring 101: jacksempowerment.com
- Business Collaboration With Jack Lookman - jacksempowerment.com
- Jaaloo Puzzles - jaaloopuzzles.com
- Curated Business Ideas - curatedbusinessideas.com

40. Social media:

Some of our Social media platforms are:

Facebook - Jack Lookman - Facebook profile - https://www.facebook.com/jack.lookman.3

Facebook group: Curated Business Ideas

Youtube channel: Curated Business Ideas

Youtube channel: Jack Lookman: https://youtube.com/@jacklookman

TikTok: jacklookman4

LinkedIn: Olayinka Carew aka Jack Lookman

41. Our books could be found at:

Amazon: - amazon.co.uk - search for Jack Lookman

Selar: https://selar.co/m/jacklookman

Or other reputable book shops.

42. OTHER PUBLICATIONS BY JACK LOOKMAN LIMITED

1. *Despair, Submission, Faith and Hope – Volume 1*

2. *Despair, Submission, Faith and Hope – Volume 2*

3. *Monetising Digital Book Reviews*

4. *E-Commerce For Traditional African Attires*

5. *Basic Management And Fundraising Tip For Community Groups*

6. *Monetising A Digital Library*

7. *Ajo, The App And Opportunities*

8. *Empowering Orphans, Widows and Widowers*

9. *Submission, Gratitude, Faith and Hope*

10. *Oro Ishiti- Indelible Yoruba Words - Adebanji Osanyingbemi*

11. *Eid Monetisation by Leveraging Technology*

12. *What are your thoughts? What is your mindset? - Volume 1*

13. *What are your thoughts? What is your mindset? - Volume 2*

14. *Twenty Curated Business Ideas - Volume 1*

15. *Jaaloo Puzzles - Volume 1*

16. *Jaaloo Puzzles - Volume 2*

43. About Jack Lookman

Olayinka Carew, aka Jack Lookman is the 1st of 5 Children.
He has 3 children, and an elderly mum. He is resident in the United Kingdom and is of Nigerian origin.

He studied at King's College, Lagos and University of Lagos.
He has varied life and work experiences.
He has been involved in voluntary and paid jobs.
He is dedicating the rest of his life to empowering and inspiring generations.
This is one of his legacy projects.
Though he has health challenges, he does not let that impede his mission and vision.
Even though he studied Engineering in University; his calling is so many miles away from that. He is currently an Entrepreneur, Content Creator, Affiliate Marketer, Volunteer, Business Collaborator and Mentor.

He is the Director and Owner of Jack Lookman Limited, a registered business in the United Kingdom; and their aim is to empower and inspire generations by leveraging the internet.

This is Jack Lookman signing off.

Thank you very much for your time.

Ire o (I wish you blessings)
Ire kabiti (I wish you loads of blessings)

www.ingramcontent.com/pod-product-compliance
Lightning Source LLC
Chambersburg PA
CBHW070937290526
45795CB00003B/1045